"Heavenly bodies are nests of invisible birds."

~ *Dejan Stojanovic, 'The Creator'*

Also by Candice James

The Depth of the Dance *(Silver Bow Publishing)* 2023
Behind the One-Way Mirror *(Silver Bow Publishing)* 2022
The Call of the Crow *(Silver Bow Publishing)* 2021
he Path of Loneliness *(Inanna Publications)* 2020
Rithimus Aeternam *(Silver Bow Publishing)* 2019
Haiku Paintings *(Silver Bow Publishing)* 2019
The 13th Cusp *(Silver Bow Publishing)* 2018
Fhaze-ing *(Silver Bow Publishing)* 2018
The Water Poems   *(Ekstasis Editions)* 2017
Short Shots   *(Silver Bow Publishing)* 2016
City of Dreams   *(Silver Bow Publishing)* 2016
Merging Dimensions   *(Ekstasis Editions)* 2015
Colors of India   *(Xpress Publications India)* 2015
Purple Haze   *(Libros Libertad)* 2014
A Silence of Echoes   *(Silver Bow Publishing)* 2014
Shorelines   *(Silver Bow Publishing*) 2013
Ekphrasticism   *(Silver Bow Publishing)* 2013
Midnight Embers   *(Libros Libertad)* 2012
Bridges and Clouds *(Silver Bow Publishing)* 2011
Inner Heart, a Journey   *(Silver Bow Publishing*) 2010
A Split in the Water   *(Fiddlehead Poetry Books)* 1979

Atmospheres

by

Candice James

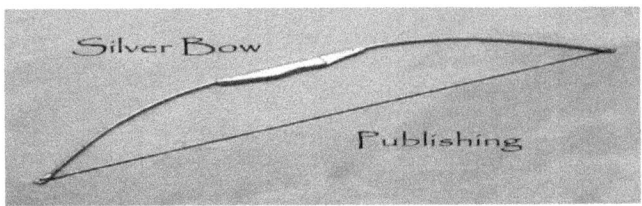

Box 5 – 720 – 6th Street,
New Westminster, BC
V3C 3C5   CANADA

Title: Atmospheres
Author: Candice James
Copyright © 2023 Silver Bow Publishing
Cover Painting: "The Faithful At Prayer" Candice James
Layout/Design: Candice James
ISBN: 9781774032596 (print)
ISBN: 9781774032602 (ebk)j

All rights reserved including the right to reproduce or translate this book or any portions thereof, in any form except for the use of short passages for review purposes, no part of this book may be reproduced, in part or in whole, or transmitted in any form or by any means, electronically or mechanically, including photocopying, recording, or any information or storage retrieval system without prior permission in writing from the publisher or a license from the Canadian Copyright Collective Agency (Access Copyright)

Library and Archives Canada Cataloguing in Publication

Title: Atmospheres / by Candice James.
Names: James, Candice, 1948- author.
Description: Poems.
Identifiers: Canadiana 2023045786X | ISBN 9781774032596 (softcover)
Classification: LCC PS8569.A429 A76 2023 | DDC C811/.6—dc23

Email: info@silverbowpublishing.com
Website: www.silverbowpublishing.com

Atmospheres

This book is dedicated to
the birdsongs that beautify the world
and all the caretakers
of the glorious winged creatures
that share their world with us.

Atmospheres

Contents

Atmospheres ... 9
Beautiful Butterfly ... 10
A Pleated Movement of Rippled Water ... 11
A Silence of Green ... 12
A Smooth Black Raven ... 13
A Thousand Bluebirds ... 14
Accumulated ... 15
Another Time, Another Space ... 16
Angels and Gulls ... 17
In the ShadOw of the Crow ... 18
Birds on a Wire ... 19
Black Satin ... 20
Coming to Rest ... 21
Conversations of Birds ... 22
The Crows We Fed ... 23
Awakening ... 24
Dying Birds ... 25
The Faithful at Prayer ... 26
Fallen Obituaries ... 27
Feathered Friends ... 28
Fly Away ... 29
Frail Sparrow ... 30
Green Memory ... 31
Jagged Poems and Bruised Teardrops ... 32
Knowing Loneliness ... 33
Orphaned Nights ... 34
Poem to the Sea ... 35
Pop-Up Ravens ... 36
Ravens and Teardrops ... 37
Sculped Crow ... 38
Silence of the Crows ... 39
The Snow Falls ... 40
Somewhere ... 41
Call of the Crow ...42

The Raven and I ... 43
The Raven Listens ... 44
The Space Between Moments ... 45
Under a Tent of Trees ... 46
Where Have All the Seagulls Gone ... 47
November Birds ... 48
White Water Rapids ...49
Echoes of an Eagle ... 50
Alone ... 51
Birds of Prey ... 52
Seeking an Empty Nest ... 53
Satin Feathers ... 54
The Crows and I ... 55
The Seagull's Cry ... 56
White Swans at Midnight ... 57
The Wishing Tree ... 58
Black Cat ... 59
Bluebirds and Lilac Butterflies ... 60
The Eagle Has Landed ... 61
I Call Out to the Crows ... 62
I Drift and Dream ...63
Just Beyond the Gray ... 64
Raven's Wing ... 65
A Deadly Splash of Green ... 66
Birds of Paradise ... 67
Dragonfly ... 68
White Swans Circling ... 69
Tall Tale ... 70
A Bird in Flight ... 71
The Brilliant Face of Time ... 72
Heartbeat of Existence ... 73
A Murder of Crows ... 74

Author Profile ... 75

Atmospheres

I watch the water strider
        skating across the autumn lake,
              elegant, wistful
at home on its watery highway of dreams.

I see the mosquitoes
        bobbing and hovering
              over stale rain puddles
                      oblivious, unaware
              on ever-changing slices of air.

I hear the warblers
        chatting incessantly
              trading comments and secrets
        harmonizing the rustle of leaves
              in the dance of the branches.

We are earth striders
        walking across the sands of time
              fingerprinting our footsteps
onto the disappearing illusions of life.

Water striders, mosquitoes,
        warblers and earth striders
              all sharing the same atmosphere
                  in the catch
            of God's exhaled breath.

Beautiful Butterfly

The butterfly followed me along the shoreline.
A beautiful butterfly of colorful design.
How odd, I thought, on a day so hot,
that a butterfly would follow the blue water line.

It started to flutter to and fro,
with every step, each stop and go.
Mostly drifting on my right hand side
as I walked the shallows of the incoming tide.

As the day grew weary and I traveled on
I thought that butterfly would be long gone;
but alas it steadfastly stayed at my side
as I walked the shallows of the incoming tide.

I walked and I whispered to that butterfly
Of memories and dreams and days gone by.
I was certain it was more than a mere insect
as it seemed to command my deepest respect.

And then it hit me out of the blue.
Perhaps it was Karma and someone I knew.
I began humming a familiar song;
a hint of your essence sidled along.

A beautiful butterfly followed me home.
I knew you were here. I wasn't alone.
Now each day I walk along the shoreline,
my beautiful butterfly soft on my mind

A Pleated Movement of Rippled Water

In a pleated movement of rippled water
I saw God sewing the earth to the sky.

And now I search for that first point of puncture;
      that golden needle mark
tattooed on the lip of a drifting horizon.

With crows on my shoulders
and stars in my eyes
I climb into the maze
of a sleeping shaman's dream
where slices of time
lay scattered in space.

      Laying claim
to my own predestined slice of time
I ride on a shoulder of crows
threading the eye of the needle
into the pleated movement of rippled water
      where God speaks to me
    in the infinite language of crows.

A Silence of Green

The frayed green fabric of the patio swing
dances in eight-six rhythm,
waltzing sporadically with the breeze.

An enraptured audience
of scattered pine cones
and rust coloured needles
sit in silent awe:
    Mesmerized,
        unable to applaud.
      Paralyzed
by the strange magic of this rhythm.

A worn broom
leans against a cobwebbed shed,
blindly staring at an overgrowth
of tall scrawny weeds
climbing the aged fence,
entangled in ivy vines.

An orange tabby cat purring,
and sparrows twittering
are the only sounds breaking the silence.

Even the fluttering
of the frayed green fabric
on the patio swing
is too soft to be heard
in this deep, bold
silence of green.

A Smooth Black Raven

The sun burns into ebony embers.
The moon turns inside out.
and basks in a twilight neon sky.

There is a stir of dark whispers
feathering beneath an overhang
of rustling, swaying branches.
A smooth black raven
conjures up invisible magicians
to recreate yesterday's precious dreams.

In the lush velvet underbelly
of this pastel tranquility
          wishes are granted
            and dreams come true.
Opaque plates of glass slide over each other
    and etch their image and essence
  onto a twilight neon jukebox
      of waxed jazz recordings
        of the third kind.

In the solace of a crimson heartbeat,
    smooth black raven
pushes the shiny gold button,
 unzips the pristine dream
    and the music plays.

A Thousand Bluebirds

The sky unzips.
    A thousand bluebirds emerge
        to ride the wind and sea.

    The rocks and trees
    sing of old mysteries
        that rest in the eider down
of majestic dreams.

        I sit
    in a ring of bright glow
surrounded by birdsong and whispers.

    A cumulative voice of bluebirds asks me,
        "What most are you?"

        I reply
"I am the hours and minutes
    of all my days."

"I am a living breathing poem
    writing my words
        onto the pages of life."

    "This is
    what most I am...
a living breathing poem."

The bluebirds understand.
They chortle softly
then slowly fly away

Accumulated

The accumulated mind of crow,
            calls to me
                    in tones
                            soft and low,
                  in the shift and shine
            of gathering moon glow.

And I am left to wonder
                why I left the fold
            The path I chose to fly was wrong;
            And now I'm lost in sorrow's song.

In the accumulated mind of here
            the dense fog this
                then finally clears.

Sense to sky and ear to ground
                I listen for the sweet of sound.
            I pray to hear the crow calls:
                to guide me home where I belong
;   accumulated in their song.

Atmospheres

Another Time, Another Space

Driving down King George Highway
    wipers slapping time
        to a song from yesterday
playing on the jukebox in my mind.

The swish of tires on the rain slicked streets
        takes me back
to the wet of my childhood.

Breakwaters, sandbars, swimming, water-skiing,
speedboats, sailboats, rowboats, and canoes.

    The calls of the birds:
        Ravens and egrets.
        Pelicans and sandpipers.
        Seagulls and crows.

    The splash of the waves:
Sun and surf.   Wind and rain.
Smiles and tears.   Joy and pain.
        You and I.

Driving down King George Highway
heading to Crescent Beach,
    as the crow flies,
        dreaming of
            another time,
            another space.

Angels and Gulls

My angels and gulls know me.
They wish me well, time and time again,
arriving ... and departing.

I have languished beneath warm, pale August moons
among tall grasses at the edge of the strand,
and held my breath to hear the gulls breathing;
to feel their hearts beating in unison with mine.

I have become one with the gulls
flying high above my sleeping body on the strand.

I have soared with them
over the slick surface of glassy rivers
leaving the scar of my wingtips on the water.

And I have lingered
beneath ice-cold December moons,
wrapped in burnt sienna,
and drowned in the aftertaste
of triple sec and dry white wine.

I have been alive for ten thousand years.
I inhale; I live; I laugh; I participate.

I have been dead for ten thousand years:
I exhale; I expire; I weep; I sleep.

My name has been read from the scrolls
        Time and time again.
    My angels and gulls know me.
The same ones are always there to greet me,
        arriving.....and departing.

In the Shadow of the Crow

A paddle-wheeler
    slices the water,
        spinning a web of dreams,
            at the edge of the Fraser River.

    A lonely crow flies overhead,

    At the edge of yesterday
        I look into a child's eyes
            and see myself.

      Today dissolves
          into yesterday's echo.

      The child transforms
          into the adult.

      The moment fades
          into a haze of dreams.

        I stand beside myself
      in the shadow of the crow.
      spinning a web of dreams
        I can call my own.

Birds on a Wire
(a sonnet)

You touch my soul like blazing prairie fire
and windblown dew upon a desert rose.
Our wings, electric ravens on a wire,
tips rapt in passion as it sparks and glows.
The wire song pierces deep into our hearts;
it's mystic rhythm holds us in a trance.
Inside these sacred canyons music starts.
We are the lovers destined for this dance
inside lust's rhapsody of precious song.
Locked safely in each other's warm embrace,
our feathers soft and yet our wings are strong,
engulfed in flames we'll vanish with no trace.

Birds on a wire with burnt electric wings:
Electrocution savoured as love sings.

Black Satin

The black satin brush
of a raven's wing
paints a narrow staircase
in my mind
where hopes, dreams and illusions
wind in spiraling patterns
of laughter and tears;
resounding and echoing
throughout the years.

A rainbow dances
across the moon's face.
Star shadows fall
through midnight's embrace.

The black satin brush
of the Raven's wing
is painting my pathway home
in a hush of whispers
and a splash of colours

The black satin brush.
The star shadowed hush.
Enfolded in the Raven's wing,
I listen to the angels sing

Coming To Rest

A Raven, slick as a black patent shoe,
        floats on calm water
    across my lake of dead dreams
        waiting to be resurrected
by the call of the wind
        and the tap, tap, tapping
    of persistent talons
disturbing the pale blue silence of my mind.

A door turns into a tapestry,
    into a curtain, a window
        then shatters
    into a dead dream resurrecting
in pearl moonbeams and pastel rainbows.

A freshly peppered wind and I
dash through a seasoned landscape
that's home to lost angels

        The slick black Raven
            caws overhead
              circles
    then comes to rest on my left shoulder.

In this magical moment of surreal rebirth
        my bones unlace
            and my flesh dissolves.

I come to rest in the eyes of the Raven.
    In the death of the breath
        I've relinquished..

Conversations of Birds

Gone are the days
of the world's kind indifference
All of it is gone
and the supple ears of my pen
have succumbed to a metal deafness.

My heart is a hand
reaching out
to find the familiar contour
of a forgotten soul.

The conversations of birds
still linger in the damp of tree branches
under a frail canopy of fog

I hear them weeping and whispering ...

Gone are the days
of the world's kind indifference
and soon the conversations of birds
will only be a memory.

The Crows We Fed

Straw dogs and scarecrow clouds
        flailing in the wind
whispered of impending rains
           that coiled green
                in a sky of hungry birds
        as we stood in awe
     feeding the crows
while the world was drowning
      and we were pulling
           away from each other.

In the back up and push
           of dying love
      a swell of tears rode high
on the shallows of an insincere kiss.

I saw your eyes flash in heaven's mirror
      for a moment in time:
in the heartbeat of an eternity;
      and I suddenly realized
        all the years we spent together
           trying to sew the earth to the sky
                were only in vain.

The crows we so casually fed
        have picked those years clean
           and all that's left
      are hungry straw dogs
           and tattered scarecrow clouds
                adrift on yesterday's tears
        and your eyes flash no more.

Awakening

I will awaken the doves
that lay sleeping on this page
and walk across the burning embers
     of yesterday

A ring of angels will form overhead
and witness the burning of my soul
and the crimson staining of my heart.

I will polish the burnished edge of a star
     that it may wax brighter.

  Then
      the doves and angels
           will sing in unison again.

Dying Birds

I saw them overhead.
White doves flying in frantic formation
      hard against the wind
chased by a posse of angry blackbirds.

      There was no escape
      They were marked
      for death

         They were tiring,
    slowing down
easy prey for the hardy crows

Clouds turned grey
against a fading horizon.
Fog fell over the mountains.
The doves crashed onto the rocks
and fell to death
in a clatter of broken wings
and dead hearts

White Doves,
      in the wrong place
      at the wrong time...

           dying birds
        killed by a murder of crows.

The Faithful at Prayer

It is not their way to kneel.

    Instead,
    they stand at full attention,
        these trees
        in full leafy salute
        paying homage
            to heaven.

The breeze
    blowing through their branches
    whispers of their unshakable faith
        into the cosmic consciousness
        they are so closely connected to.

Invisible rainbows
    and angels' tears
        anoint the faithful at prayer

        and the doves in attendance
           sing
        a silent a chorus
        of hallelujah
        that echoes gently
           inside
        the fabric of forever.

Fallen Obituaries

Thunder
      rolls
           then roars
and curls over the mountains
      in fading echoes.

We are dying birds
      amidst a rant of ravens.

      We can no longer fly.
      Our wings are broken.
           We are fast becoming
           smudged obituaries;
fragments and bits
of shrunken souls
      that no longer fit.

We fall into death
      in the wake of decayed stars;
           fallen obituaries
drowning in sleet and rain.

      Lightning cracks
      every time we die.

Feathered Friends

Tiny creatures swooping low.
Wingtips grazing feathered petals.
    Bachelor Button flowers
    touched by breeze and bird.

    Wind kissed,
        sun blown.

Nestled in nature`s embrace,
    we are all
        kindred spirits.

Fly Away

The wistful gaze
of the red breasted warbler
witnessing sleepy trees
baring their branches
to nature's motherly prodding.

Grass and leaves,
scatter in gusting winds.
Winter's icy touch
rocks Autumn's child
in a fragile cradle of twigs.
  The robin laments
  the last kiss of Fall
as it rushes into Winter's embrace.

The crisp crackle of dried leaves
under feather light claws
echoes of endless flight.
A few more steps on familiar ground,
the Robin's small breath fogs the air.

  In seasonal spin,
  far away suns
  and familiar warm skies
  parade through his mind
  like gypsy whispers
  promising sweeter sunsets.

Out of a cool gray night,
into bright sunlight,
to a far away land and new day,
  the Robin flies away.

Frail Sparrow

I peer from behind the rock
and the frail Sparrow
      lifts its head,
        looks around,
aware of something there
that wasn't there before.

I watch its delicate dance on the lawn
graceful, magical,,
elegant, majestic.

Slowly the Sparrow
moves from the grass
to the rain puddle;
softly sips the wet.

I watch in awe
at the beautiful painting
unfolding before my eyes:
Splendid, peaceful creatures,
gliding through God's vast blue sky,
drifting across nature's green canvas.

I move from behind the rock.
the frail

      lifts its head
      looks around
              and flies away ...
        just flies, flies
               away.

Green Memory

Crows don't forget.
    They posture and caw.
    They coddle and jive.
        They jostle and rhyme
        in their own cadent time.

    Coal wings,
        ebony eyes,
            birds loaded for bear
            inside a green memory.

They hunker down in the trees of my dreams
tearing the ragged edge off their seams.

        Crows
            calling my name;
    calling, calling my name
            over and over again.

        They don't want me to forget
the days we flew together
in the swing and sway
of our own private murder,
        knifing our way through
        sun swept days and sacred rain
            in a vibrant green memory.

        Crows keep calling my name.
            Crows don't forget.

Jagged Poems and Bruised Teardrops

I dance on a frayed high wire,
    high above a jagged poem,
        perched on the edge
            of a fallen feather
from a fleeing swallow's trembling wing.

I pivot on the wet slick of a bruised teardrop
    falling from the eye
        of a migrant bird
        emerging from
            the dark side of my soul.

I falter, sidestep, and pirouette
    through signs in the stars and the moon
        into the beautiful ballet
            you wrote for me
            to shine in.

The dance has ended.
    The angel has touched down.
        The migrant bird has landed.

I sit in silence
    polishing jagged poems
    and bruised teardrops
        to decorate your eyes ...

    that you may find me again
        when the swallows return.

Knowing Loneliness

An old tree
          with broken branches.

    A bird
              with no song.

    They share a moment in time

          knowing
          loneliness.

Orphaned Night

The cry of a seagull,
and a whisper of waves tugs at my sleeve
in the sleeping sway of a high noon sun.
The waves are wet sapphires
dancing with diamonds and dreams
and in my reverie, you return to me.

Your eyes are burnt into the heart of my hours.
and the dreams I cage torment the orphaned night
as it hunkers down on a beach too far.

The cry of a seagull, a whisper of waves
and the shocking blue edge of steel blunted stars
coax the razor of dark to cut through the fading day.
A murder of minutes and crows
adrift on the broken wings of time
track slowly away from this familiar shoreline.
The sun swings into a sordid dark room,
fondles the air in a vacuum of nerves,
as a rampaging madness invades the sky;
and all my days become an asylum
in the ticking tock of a clockwork twilight.

Locked in the tightening embrace
of the lonely, orphaned night
the minutes and crows fly from my lips.
and the burnt-out hours die in my eyes;

You are lost, lost to me forever
and all that remains is
the cry of a seagull, a whisper of waves
and the lonely, orphaned night.

Poem to the Sea

You plant shells on damp shores
            to brighten the landscape:
    shiny abalone,
        mother of pearl
                and creations
            scattered amongst the pebbles;
    agates and driftwood
nestled in with the cracked shells
            and frayed feathers
      nudged up against the logs.

All shaped by the movement
        of a million waves
             and polished by the current.

    I spend an eternity watching
        these small sea treasures
          polish the white spine
         of a frayed feather
    fallen from a long-dead seagull's wing.

        So soft, it's still adrift
        on the ghostly stardust
        of a long-lost dream.

Pop-Up Ravens

I lie on a wet blanket
            of smooth diamond water.
I float
      closer and closer
           to the smoky wish
      I see fading into the ebbing horizon.

Pop-up ravens
      dance on the lip
           of a starlit skyline.

Crashing headlong
      through fading ribbons of sunlight,
           I can almost hear them
                calling my name.

As I drift on my blanket
      of smooth diamond water
           I can hear them
           asking me questions.

            The one thought in my mind:

            How to answer them
              in pop-up poems
            they can understand.

Ravens and Teardrops
(a villanelle)

On the soft silk of a black Raven's wing
a haunting melody this way came.
The teardrops pooled in a watery ring.
A feather fell from a rainbow string.
I thought I saw it write my name
on the soft silk of a black Raven's wing.
I said "Look here. See the treasures I bring."
I witnessed the feather burst into flame.
The teardrops pooled in a watery ring.
In the distance an angel began to sing
shedding stardust and gold from its frame,
onto the silk of a black Raven's wing.
On the downside of wing I clutch and cling
as the Raven lays claim to dissolving fame.
The teardrops pool in a watery ring.
Across the sky a feeling is stealing
to erase every last bit of sin and shame.
On the soft silk of a black Raven's wing
the teardrops pool in a watery ring.

Sculpted Crow

Aloof,
taking refuge in small talk,
I hide inside my drink.
Surfing the amber tide on slick ice cubes,
I hang ten on the ninth wave of boredom rolling in
and laugh when expected to.

I whisper to the sculpted crow in the corner.
I whisper of mustache wax and bubble gum dreams
unravelling on sugar glazed strings.
Perched on the tenth wave of boredom
he listens only half-heartedly.

On evenings like these
I strain to hear the sounds of silence.
I search to find the edge of this evening,
to climb out and zip it inside its own pocket.

I long to run away
from the smell of small talk and boredom.
I want to laugh because I feel like it,
not because I'm expected to.

I lift my glass
and silently toast
the insanity of it all.

The sculpted crow in the corner smiles.

Silence of the Crows

In the silence of the crows
there is a slick ice-line of tears
that hangs in melting mist
on the frosty exhalation
of a sleeping forest's breath.

The white of the frost
and the black of the crows
paint a frayed checkerboard pattern
in a scatter of licorice nibs
        and sugar cubes.

I walk through this thick silence
bundled in my own atmosphere
warmed by the layered fleece
        of my mind,
deafened by the unwritten music
that cries for release in my brain
and rattles the raw edge
        of my nerves.

I walk deeper into the forest
searching for my comfort zone
and the elusive peace I crave.

I find the solace I seek
in the silence of the crows.

The Snow Falls

The snow falls:
    tiny, shredded flakes of shiny tinsel
    swirling in the moonbeam shafting

        d
          o
            w
              n

        onto my face.

The shoreline
    on the other side of the river
        shimmers
    against a dissolving horizon.

And somewhere,
deep inside this winter night,
    I hear a lonesome bird
        crying through the chill.

    And the snow falls ...
      wetter now
        with the weight
          of that lonesome bird's cry.

Somewhere

There is dust on the branches,
      rust on the leaves
and a forest alive with black satin wings.

    I sit in a separate space
bereft of time, beneath a dappled sky,
    content in my makeshift mind.

      A lost and disoriented crow
      sways in a crippled poplar
      surrounded by evergreens.

   I hear the crow whisper,
beckoning me deeper into the forest.

I start to crumble, like the ancient relic I am,
      into the dust of my bones,
        rust of my heart
and the black satin of the dream closing in.

Exhaling my final breath,
I hear a flurry of wings
and the hazy call of the crow,
as the dream breaks
into a deluge of bittersweet memories.

And somewhere...
somewhere a cedar tree growing roses
rests on a desert dune of melting snow
     where a crow whispers
into the black satin dream I am dreaming.

Call of the Crow

A phantom mist wisps and swirls,
rolls and tumbles then touches down
to tango with the evergreen trees
on the slick rhythm of the wind.

Yellow glints of sunlight,
hiding behind a sapphire patchwork quilt,
try to wheel and spike their way
through the damp leaves
and a residue of ghostly ravens;

Their caws wax and wane
in pale ochre shafts of luminescence
reflecting a dimming surreal dreamscape.
In this endless expanse of forest
and sway of branches
a small village of ravens
has fallen asleep in their own private Nirvana,

Falling from the soft shoulders
of the whirling, swirling mist.
a sheer veil of memories
shawls over the sleeping birds
resonating softly in a stir of harmonies
before they dissolve under a perceived rain.

Twilight whets its lips,
opens its gaping maw,
unleashes its indigo breath
and slowly swallows
the last remnants of light ...
silencing the call of the crow
until the crack of dawn.

The Raven and I

A wayward star glistens
on the whetted lips of a wanton breeze.

Across a pale-yellow sky
an ebony raven sits astride
the wind's coat tails,
riding slices of shadow
and shimmer,
spinning haphazardly
at the edge of encroaching night.

I, too, spin haphazardly
on a torn and tossed renegade wind
dissolving in the misty tears
       of a dying sun.

    The raven and I...
        both of us
  old beyond our years.

The Raven Listens

Leaves fall from trees like crepe paper wool
in the afterglow of Nature's pull.
Reflections peek through this gentle shine
on waters turned to splendid wine.
Sparkling Chardonnay flows through my mind.
Light spools and pools then starts to unwind.

> *And all the while the river glistens;*
> *all the while the raven listens.*

Perchance I may see an eagle fly by;
and perhaps a tear may fall from his eye.
Autumn leaves in full state of undress
lay patiently waiting for fall to confess
she's fallen prey to winter's charms
and seeks the comfort of his arms.

> *And all the while a snowflake glistens;*
> *all the while the raven listens.*

I watch not sands in the hourglass;
nor care I for the hours that pass.
I lay with my ear pressed to the ground
in silence listening for the sound
of footfalls whispering you're returning.
as I wait for you here sighing and yearning.

> *And all the while a teardrop glistens;*
> *all the while the raven listens.*

The Space Between Moments

A lonely seagull cries and careens
      above the ocean's shimmering face.

    A ghostly tailor
          weaves the jagged shore
              to the waterline
              buttoning the sun
                  to the ocean's face,
                mirroring the moment
            into an eternity of sorts
        somewhere inside a distorted corner
of time's hazy dimension.

    From my perch on the shore
        I watch the freedom of the seagull.

Somewhere in the space between moments
        we share
            a kindred breath.

Under a Tent of Trees

I lay beneath the drums of heaven
stoking the thunder in the clouds,
safe from the wet,
under a tent of leafy trees
as my mind bends the fabric of time.

>Snowflakes drift idly by,
>just beyond the breeze.

>Summer's gone
>and so are summer dreams.

>Childhood's gone
>and so are childish things.

A small covey of pigeons
wings by on a prayer and a sigh
in perfect synchronicity
with the drums of heaven.

I lay under a tent of trees
    waiting, waiting ...
to take eternity's hand.

Atmospheres

Where Have All the Seagulls Gone?

Swimming in dreams at night
    on waves of pleasure and pain
I dip my heart into a bright shiny ripple
    and find my other self
        singing a song of six-pence
            inside a pocket of rye.

    All around me
a ring of blackbirds are circling high,
    resplendent against a turquoise sky
    and overhead by a murder of crows
        watching me like a hawk.

And I wonder:
    where have all the seagulls gone?
This is an ocean, not a river.
    The smells of the sea
        intoxicate the breeze
    where my other self sits
    knitting her thoughts together
on the brow of a distant hill only she sees.

I sit in my bright shiny ripple.
    She hides in her pocket of rye;
        Both of us wondering ...
    Where have all the seagulls gone?

And all the while
    the blackbirds and crows whisper
of kings and queens and pie and rye.

        Once upon a time
        there used to be seagulls.

November Birds

November birds
        sigh midnight chirps
                into thick fog.

    Muted cries, calling,
        fall on deaf ears.
    Lost hearts, beating,
        break on desolate shores.

        Loneliness,
aching,
desperation
        penetrate
        this fog
            like a silver spike
                piercing
            the eye of midnight.

I will polish and bronze
        these November birds
            in my mind ...

    Lest I forget this loneliness.

Atmospheres

White Water Rapids

The white water rapids, frothing and foaming.
The slick black rocks. moaning and groaning.
      The west wind howling.
      The wood jamb growling
like a wild rabid dog, chasing a log
        down a slippery crack
          on the river's back.

The white water rapids gurgle and scream
in the tight choke hold of man and machine.
      D.An eagle flies by
        with selective eye.
It swoops and dips, claws and wing tips,
        diving and wishing
          for old time fishing.

Once long ago there were birch bark canoes,
totem poles, ponies and moccasin shoes
        imprinting the shore.
        But that was before
machinery and dredges tore down mountain ledges,
          in this twilight noon
          of things done too soon.

        An eagle drifts across the sky.
        A teardrop falls from his eye.

    Once, there were birch bark canoes ...

Echoes of an Eagle
(a villanelle)

Against an opalescent purple sky
starlight flickers in the twilight glow
in echoes of an eagle flying by.
High above the lovers as they lie
aflame inside the fire that burns below
against an opalescent purple sky.
If they had wings they would surely fly
within this song that whispers soft and low,
in echoes of an eagle flying by.
Wrapped in the essence of a sacred sigh
Cupid bows his head and rests his bow
against a purple opalescent sky.
Angels throng in murmurs and draw nigh.
Wings of gossamer and stardust flow
in echoes of an eagle flying by.
Inside an antique pocket full of rye
a nursery rhyme resounds from long ago
against a purple opalescent sky
in echoes of an eagle flying by.

Alone

Why was that bird crying
in the middle of the night?

        Eleven o'clock,
    one hour before midnight
and I know I heard a bird crying.

In late November,
I heard a bird cry
        in the middle of the night
        in the middle of my life
            and I knew ...

        I wasn't alone.

The Birds of Prey

A Nightingale's copper voice sang in the trees
Serenading angels gliding on the breeze.
A lonely Robin's song announced the end of fall.
Winter heard its voice and came running to its call.

Under a haloed sky of approaching winter dawn,
at sunrise in the forest glade a mother and her fawn.
Carved into a cedar tree, a woodpecker's profile,
a beautiful acrylic painting in a surreal style.

Then the birds of prey flew wingless overhead
chanting in soft choruses to the newly dead.
And I was wont to say the measure of the things I saw:
Bits of skeletons that caused the Crows to caw.

A nightingale's copper voice echoed through the sky.
The birds of prey were sad but they could not cry.
They flew tearless high above, hearts engorged with pity.
They flew wingless disappearing from this winter city.

Seeking an Empty Nest

Above the ridge, the dark night ebbs and flows
    staring me down with twinkling eyes
        through a painted ebony blanket.

I stand in rags silk clothing
    in a pool of ink-stained water
        wet with the knowledge of stars.

Wearing a heart of crimson roses
    invisible amid the bloodstained sky
I pass through the face of a rippling mirror
    where my shattered dreams
        await the glue-master's brush
    for a miracle in the making.

My icy soul rises into the kiss
    of a dark raven flying above.

    I'm reborn and baptized
        in a sanctified rain;
            I emerge
                a crow with wet feathered wings
        lost in the deep dark secret of night
seeking an empty nest
    that I can call home.

Satin Feathers

We're wrapped in the satin feathers
        we fashioned from our broken wings.
        We will fly no more
        to the songs of old.
                We will dance no more
                to the lies we told.

The weave of our careless words
        chokes like a noose around our necks
        and robs us of the will to speak.

Robbed of our songs and lies
        we hobble away from each other
        down a dusty road of wounds and scars
        that once was a bed of satin feathers.

        The songs of old have worn away
        and the dance floor is warped and broken...

                Flightless birds
                We fly no more.

The Crows and I

Beneath a darkening sky
        I hunker down on a solid branch
                in dark sacrosanct prayer
        with the crows of midnight's passage
     waiting for the shimmering needle of moonlight
        to sew our thoughts together.

The fluttering of prayer rises in my throat
        and comes to rest on ebony wings
and a deep knowing the crows understand
        resonates in the echoes of this surreal forest.

The wind rustles the branches
        like metal brushes on a snare drum;
an orchestra section of leaves comes alive
        in a woodwind symphony of sound,

        Its staccato and legato etch messages
              onto the black sable coat of night
            chaining her kiss to the wind
        wounding the sky with the cut of her lips
as strange songs seep from the needle of moonlight
        in slow-motion retrograde rhythm
            and indecipherable lyrics
        that only the crows and I understand.

The Seagull's Cry

A solitary seagull's cry
        stabs the lonely sky.

        Invisible blood spills
              from its surreal cicatrix.

        There's a living dream being drawn
           through the eye of heaven's needle.

When the seagull disappears,
        the echo of its cry
              will stain the wounded sky.

White Swans at Midnight

The white swans at midnight
shone stark in the moonlight
as we strolled holding hands
on the white silver sands.

Near those glistening birds
in the womb of our words
our hearts opened up
as we sipped from love's cup.

The world was a song
as we walked along
two stepping through time
in our own private rhyme.

Then the world shifted
and our hearts drifted.
I remember that day
when you walked away.

The white silver sands
had slipped through our hands
and the white swans at dawn
disappeared with our song.

The Wishing Tree
* Ekphrastic poem written to the painting
by Candice James and Hermine Weiss

Alone on the horizon,
attended to by birds,
the wishing tree is whispering
in poetry and words

Against a tranquil sky
she stands in still repose
above a stand of trees
nestled down below

The glowing purple rocks
whisper tales of glory
to anyone who'll listen
to their seasoned story.

And all the while the wishing tree,
whispering soft words,
relaxes in her quietude
attended to by birds.

Black Cat

Invisible confetti falling softly
      from a blurry, damp afternoon sky
wetting the slick of my thoughts,
      honing them into a pinnacled hole
to cut through the chaff of your heart;
      to find the meadow you are lying in:

            lush green fields
               as   far
            as the eye can see.

I follow the bluebirds
      and butterflies
            your ever-present familiars
             that carry the scent of you.

            I can almost taste your tears.

                I am the black cat
            you've been longing for
                 and I'm coming home
                     to you.

Bluebirds and Lilac Butterflies

I was born with a bluebird
        on my shoulder
    and lilac butterflies
        in my eyes
    and everything was beautiful,
        beautiful ...
        until it wasn't.

I walked barefoot on broken glass
    I bowed down to strangers before the mast
    and slept in the dust of hardened stars.

In the cold fell clutch of an iron fist
I was stuck in the mire of a charcoal mist
        until I wasn't.

        And now,
        as I die,
the bluebird returns to my shoulder
    and the lilac butterflies
        burn the tears from my eyes
            and everything is beautiful,
            beautiful ...
        forevermore.

The Eagle Has Landed
(Ekphrastic poem to painting by Lavana La Brey)

Fish for a carpet, the sky for a roof
two Eagles have landed long in the tooth.
A third Eagle arrives talons, dark as coal,
extended to land on the carved totem pole.

Behind the sky Eagle is the ghost of a crow
lit up in the lavender sky afterglow.
This triumvirate of Eagles is standing guard
in the northern reflections of God's back yard.

The Eagle on the stump is thinking and wishing
for big runs of Salmon and old-time fishing.
The Eagle on the wing of the totem pole
is scanning the landscape for a fox or rabbit hole.

When they've rested awhile and are re-energized
their instincts and hunger will be emphasized.
They'll take off like the regal eagles they are
their dark shadows sparkling in the shine of a star.

Mystery and folk-lore whisper through hills enchanted
deep in the Northlands where the eagle has landed.

I Call Out to the Crows

I am melting in this relentless rain
and the clouds are threatening
      to blot me out.
The stars have died at the moon's side.

And still the crows search
for the scatter of remnants
that once composed the me I used to be.

I've been robbed of my feathers
and walk cold and wet through a heavy world

I call out and reach for the scent of the crows
      both here and not here.

      I spin in place, arms flapping,
      grasping for an up-draught,
      calling out to the crows
      desperate to be found, to fly;
          but to no avail.
          I am lost ...

      I spin in place
and slowly start my journey
      toward the vanishing.

I Drift and Dream

At comfort in the shade
of Sapperton Park trees,
    listening to the crow calls,
        tuning out the jackhammers,
            car horns and sirens.

    I drift and dream
        with eyes wide open.

There is a specific handwriting
    to this lazy afternoon;
        a white scrawl
            across a pale blue sky,
        evident, yet indecipherable
        like my shadow
           on the sun streaked grass.

Once, this was a safe place.
    Now, in this age of unrest
        and random terror
I'm on edge,
    aware that I must be constantly aware
        of my surroundings.

Still, I drift and dream,
    ever vigilant, with eyes wide open.

    Things change.
        Things always change,
    but the call of the crow remains the same;
        like the whisper in my voice
    and my shadow
        on the sun-streaked grass.

Just Beyond the Gray

In the drift and grift of a gray afternoon,
waiting in the car beneath fir and elm
in the Saturday city parking lot
a rustle of ghost draws my attention.
A murder of unseen crows noisily announces
the opening of gates from another dimension.

>*It's so calm and serene,*
>*Yet, otherworldly and eerie.*

>And then through the din
>the gentle chirp of a robin
who has defeated the army of militant crows
>>with his tender song of peace.

>The trees have fallen silent.
>The world is almost asleep
>but the robin and I keep vigil,
>scanning the visible
>for the invisible.

In the drift and grift of this gray afternoon
I sit quietly, caged in my solitude,
while the robin begins to chirp
>slightly louder
waiting patiently for me to follow
>into the rustle of ghost
>>just beyond the gray.

Raven's Wing

Summer's gone.
and the songbirds no longer sing.
The shine's gone from their diamond ring
a sky of bling
and a dark foreboding Raven's wing
overshadows everything.

Autumn to fall
and then winter's pall.
The snow pelting down
onto broken ground.

This icy Winter chill
will melt and spill
into a crisp Spring sky of blue
chasing a Summer wind long overdue.

Then Summer's gone ...
but not for long.

Fall chases winter
into Spring's dawn
sprinkling her dreams
with a sky of bling
and a shiny ebony Raven's wing
accentuating everything.

A Deadly Splash of Green

There is dust on the sidewalk,
rust and yellow on the leaves
and a forest alive with
a deadly splash of green.

I sit in a separate space,
beneath a dappled blue sky.

I am a wayward poplar
surrounded by evergreens;
a cedar growing roses
on a desert dune of melting snow.

In the corner of my eye
I see a random tear dropping
from a raven's aching heart.
At the edge of my hearing
     a crow caws,
beckoning me deeper into the forest.

I start to crumble,
like the ancient relic I am,
into the dust on the sidewalk,
the rust on the leaves.

Exhaling my final breath,
    I follow the call of the crow
        into the final forest
           and
    the deadly splash of green.

Birds of Paradise

In the sacred green
    of forest and glade
        the birds of paradise
    are romancing the stone
        and calling me home ...
            calling me home.

In a brief encounter long ago,
    in violet dreams rocked to and fro
    I was one with the birds of paradise
        before the black and white
            turned to gray.

In a wonderland
    of bright white shade
        the birds of paradise
    are romancing the stone
        and calling me home ...
            calling me home.

Dragonfly (for Janet Kvammen)

Dragonfly, with intricate, patterned
spider web weave,
delicately perched on satin green stem;
the dew glistening, gleaning your wings
to a sleek, pearly shine.

Transparent wings
dip, dip dipping the lake;
skip, skip skipping the pier,
then careening upward
with long sleek body.

Riding a sunbeam, kissing the sky,
rippling the tranquility
of dampened rainbow strings.
Coaxing the music within and without,
scoring new harmonies
into nature's symmetry.
Gliding through glade,
skating on blade, sliding on currents,
swimming through air,
whispering secrets to the rain.

Mysterious and magical,
sovereign and statuesque.
Your elegance pervades
the miniature world of natural wonders.

Graceful and lithe
Balancing on the tip of God's paintbrush
Accenting Nature's masterpiece.

Dragonfly
Diva of Dance
Ballerina of Beauty.

White Swans Circling

In the core of my fleeting daydream
               butterflies, lilac and blue,
       fly through the skin of my soul
           to lay down
       in the white of my heart.

I sit on the shore of an indigo lake
        alive with white swans circling
               the darkened corners of my thoughts.

                    Whistles are blowing.
                    Ravens are crowing.
         And the swallows have come home to nest.

I open my mind to the world once again
        and the daydream drifts away
                with the butterflies in hot pursuit
        leaving a scar on the skin of my soul.

       Then the indigo lake disappears
         like a kiss that never was
       and the white swans circle no more.

Tall Tale

I ordered some cosmic soup and ate my share of crow.
I thought I had arrived but still had far to go.
I met a seagull wading and strolling on the shore.
We spoke of things and thought we'd both been here before.

We spoke of time and space and the universe divide.
We waded deeper in and spoke of time and tide.
He told me of his time in Spain and the insurrection.
I said I was with Jesus at his resurrection.

We bantered back and forth with some truth but mostly lies.
He was a regal seagull; that much I could surmise.
We talked of composition, poetry and prose
and some obscure writers no-one recalls or knows.

He said he'd been a courier before he broke his wing.
I told him I'd played football but only second string.
We'd both dabbled in painting but never learned to draw.
He said his crow wife left he because he couldn't caw.

Some pelicans were fishing at the water's edge.
An eagle perched and preened on a rocky ledge.
The seagull turned to me and said by the way my name is Dick.
I said my name's Cornelius but my friends just call me Slick.

Engrossed in conversation the time had slipped away.
The clouds were rolling in and covering up the day.
I bent down to shake his wing just before we split
and that's my tall tale story ... and I'm sure stickin' to it.

A Bird in Flight
(a villanelle)

I'm dreaming of a bird in flight
with feathers glittering with gold
lighting up the darkest night.
It dips and sways from left to right.
In the palm of midnight's hold
I'm dreaming of a bird in flight
dancing in a pool of pristine light.
It paints a picture bright and bold
lighting up the darkest night.
Inside a halo burning bright
it's disenfranchised ice and cold.
I'm dreaming of a bird in flight
inside the sweet of heaven's bite
where dreams cannot be bought or sold.
lighting up the darkest of night.
I hear an angel's voice recite
as gleaming golden wings unfold.
I'm dreaming of a bird in flight
lighting up the darkest night.

The Brilliant Face of Time

As moonlight shines the brilliant face of time
stars commence to turn it into rhyme.
That's the time the poet wanders in
and pulls the inspiration from time's skin.

I walk the shoreline in a summer haze
revisiting the realm of yesterdays
alive with egrets, terns and eagles' cries
and my heart sings inside its maudlin sighs.

I hear the lonesome howl of crying gulls,
the wind tossed ocean, as it roars and lulls,
whispering secrets to sand and seashells,
driftwood, salt air, sounds of church yard bells.

The bird of paradise has flown away
but leaves behind the darling buds of May.
I hear the sweet song of a Robin with red breast,
as I am travelling further from my rest.

Awakening from my daydream reverie
I leave behind a fading memory.
With fresh ink I inscribe a brand new rhyme
as moonlight shines the brilliant face of time.

Heartbeat of Existence

The gulls soar and dip
on the river's wet lip
as chickadees whistle
inside bush and thistle;
and the ravens fly high
in a bright sunlit sky
with precision and persistence
in the heartbeat of existence.

Dawn and dusk, sisters in silence
in the magic of constellations,
hold hands with time and tide
as I sway in sacred dance
to the pulse of consolation
in the heartbeat of existence.

A Murder of Crows
(a villanelle)

The night unzipped a bloodstained rose
and spilled tears from its ebony jar.
The sky came alive with a murder of crows.
It cracked at the seams to expose
the broken edge of a shattered star
as the night unzipped a bloodstained rose.
The essences and afterglows
of dying sparks became a scar;
and the sky came alive with a murder of crows.
Like a charcoal mist on December snows
this dream was sullied and always too far.
The night unzipped a bloodstained rose
with fragile arrows and broken bows.
In the wounded paw of a raging jaguar
my cup ran over, shattered then froze.
As I stepped back into my avatar
the night unzipped a bloodstained rose;
and the sky came alive with a murder of crows.

Candice James

Author Profile

Candice James served 2 terms (2010-2016) as Poet Laureate of New Westminster BC CANADA and was appointed Poet Laureate Emerita by the City of New Westminster in November, 2016. She is a visual artist; a musician; a singer/songwriter; a workshop facilitator , book reviewer; and the author of sixteen books of poetry. She is also co-author with Matthew Jose re the "Double Trouble poetry series Volumes 1 through 5". Her poetry has appeared in a variety of international anthologies and magazines.

Candice's artwork has appeared in many magazines internationally including Duende (Goddard University of Fine Arts, Vermont); SurVision, (Ireland); The Arts and Entertainment Magazine (Hollywood); CQ International, (New York); and Wax, Poetry Art Magazine (Canada)

She is also Founder of Royal City Literary Arts Society; Poetic Justice; Poetry in the Park; Poetry New Westminster; RCLAS Singer Songwriters; Fred Cogswell Award for Excellence in Poetry and she is the recipient of the Bernie Legge Artist Cultural Award and Pandora's Collective Citizenship Award.

For further info visit *https://en.wikipedia.org/wiki/Candice_James*
www.silverbowpublishing.com or *www.candicejames.com*

www.ingramcontent.com/pod-product-compliance
Lightning Source LLC
Chambersburg PA
CBHW060033040426
42333CB00042B/2415